I ma

Rob

1771 Highla 94

Berkeley CA

The Heart Has Its Reasons

THE HEART HAS ITS REASONS

Reflections on Sports and Life

by Bob Mitchell

To Lonnie,
with best wishes.
BM

Diamond Communications, Inc.
South Bend, Indiana
1995

THE HEART HAS ITS REASONS

Manufactured in the United States of America

10 9 8 7 6 5 4 3 2 1

DIAMOND COMMUNICATIONS, INC.
POST OFFICE BOX 88
SOUTH BEND, INDIANA 46624
(219) 299-9278
FAX (219) 299-9296

Library of Congress Cataloging-in-Publication Data

Mitchell, Robert L., 1944-
The heart has its reasons : reflections on sports & life / by Bob Mitchell.
p. cm.
ISBN 0-912083-71-9 : $18.95
1. Sports--Poetry. I. Title.
PS3563.I814H43 1995
811'.54--dc20 94-8844
CIP

For Stu Seides,
eminent cardiologist, more eminent friend.

Contents

Acknowledgments

Paraphrasing someone's quote (I think it was Yogi's: weren't they *all* Yogi's?), I'd like to thank everyone who made these poems necessary.

A tip of the cap to the following mentors, who taught me about competition, courage, and growing up during my formative years: Bill Thompson, Ernie Fleishman, Lonnie Hanauer, Jon Plaut, Larry Silver, Bob Bell, and Clarence Chaffee.

I also admired a number of early heroes who (unbeknownst to them) fueled my athletic fires: Babe Zaharias, Ben Hogan, Bob Cousy, Willie Mays, Ken Rosewall, Tony Trabert; and the lesser-known but no less impactful Bob Liss, Jon Maksik, Chuck Kaufman, and Steve Weinstock.

My thanks also to contemporaries who shared my passion for sports and who pushed me to perform beyond my expectations, as an athlete and as a person: Al Gorfin, Jimmy Blumstein, Kenny Horn, Fred Thaler, and the best tennis opponents and friends anyone could ask for, David Frantz and Alan Zahn.

Regarding the poems themselves, I am grateful to Ray Robinson, Mike Schacht, Marty Appel, Dick Schaap, George Vecsey, and Ira Berkow for their kind words of support. And most particularly to David Citino, a remarkable poet and person, who, through his encouragement and numerous insightful suggestions, helped me realize the poet within me.

Finally, a special word of thanks to my children—Noah, Jennifer, and Sarah—whose love and support through the years have made me, to misquote a certain Iron Horse, the luckiest father on the face of the earth.

FOREWORD

In the fall of 1962, Ron Tobin (then my French professor at Williams, now a friend) introduced me to the words that would prove to have a major impact on my life (and on the title of this book): *Le cœur a ses raisons, que la raison ne connaît point.*

"The heart has its reasons to which Reason is oblivious": this paradox, immortalized by the French religious writer and philosopher Blaise Pascal, struck an immediate, inner chord with its pithy expression of the conflict between heart and mind, intuition and logic, devout faith and ordered, Cartesian thought.

So much so, I guess, that twenty-four years later, as I was being rushed on a gurney to bypass surgery, I am told that I quoted it in French to my anesthesiologist.

And more recently, as I was writing these poems, Pascal's words once again surfaced involuntarily: I realized that much of what was coming out had to do with the spontaneous, mysterious, "heart-driven" side of sports that creates a sense of awe and joy in both spectator and participant.

This is not to dismiss the other, left-brain side: far from it. Strategy, planning, and thinking are, of course, all part of the act of competing. (Just read anything Ted Williams ever wrote about the art of hitting!)

But the thrill and the magic of sports result, to a great extent, from the unreasoning side of human experience. From instinct, intuition, atavism, and emotion. From the production of adrenalin under duress. From creativity born from the loins of surprise and unpredictability. From irrational hope in the midst of desperation. (Is it mere coincidence that the song from *Damn Yankees* isn't entitled "Ya Gotta Have Brain"?) From the inner workings of the gut and the development of private passions. From the nostalgia and memories that accrue during a lifetime. And from the life-lessons that endow the sporting *moment* with a far greater significance than it might ostensibly appear to have.

Many of the poems are extremely personal (and thus, I hope, extremely universal): as for so many millions of people, sports has occupied a very special place in my heart. It provided me with heroes during those tough early years. It gave me self-esteem and that wonderful ability to feel good any time I put on a mitt, swung a racquet or club, threw a ball (of any kind), or competed at *anything*. It taught me to appreciate the importance of the intangibles: passion, patience, pride, tenacity, humility, courtesy, honesty, limits, moderation, focus. It allowed me to meet my wife of twenty-six years and represented a common bond between me and my children. It brought me closer to some of my closest friends. And it's still one of the reasons I look forward to getting up every morning.

I've been writing these poems probably since I was four. And after forty-five years of incubation, I guess they just popped out. (Like they say, you can't hurry love.) They represent a few of the heartfelt thoughts, theories, inquiries, lessons, mysteries, quandaries, and memories that the experience of sports has allowed me to harbor, develop, ponder, profit from, ruminate on, struggle with, and cherish. And they pay homage to some of the athletes who have—by their talent and charisma—left within me a lasting cardiological imprint.

Merci, Blaise.

The Heart Has Its Reasons

Lessons

The Heart Has Its Reasons

Le cœur a ses raisons, que la raison ne connaît point;
on le sait en mille choses.
—Blaise Pascal

The great appeal of sports:
magic thought to be practiced
only by superstars
is actually accessible to the general public!

From klutz to accomplished athlete,
we've all felt that moment
when the brain shuts down
and the body follows the dictates
of some weird, wonderful force.

It comes from the heart,
atavistic instinct as natural
as a dog's leg twitching
while his belly's being rubbed.
And arrives unexpectedly,
often when we are,
like some cornered beast,
in the direst of straits.

And then—ZING!—this strange thing happens,
bringing with it a feeling that somehow
we are a race of fallen angels,
capable of performing
short-lived, sporadic, but undeniable God-like deeds.

Caught at the service line while charging the net,
in a split instant we perform the miraculous,
lunging, sprawling reflex-stab-angled-drop-half-volley
that dies in the noonday clay.
For a fleeting instant,
as we look down,
our forearm has metamorphosed into

The Rocket's sledgehammer,
our wrist has the supple, soft genius
of Johnny Mac.

Or,
seeing the peg from short
heading for sure disaster into the dirt,
something orders our head to look away,
our right arm to cross over our body,
and, like some hawk picking off
a trout in mid-flight,
we perform The Perfect Short-Hop
that would make Gil or Keith proud.

Or,
sensing,
to our left and way out of peripheral range,
a teammate streaking hoopward,
we somehow summon the
spinning-bounce-hook-pass-between-two-defenders.
Hitting our man on the dead run for an easy two,
we suddenly feel,
just this once,
what Cooz and Oscar and Jerry and Hondo and Clyde and
Larry and Magic and Michael
must have felt a million times.

The heart has its reasons for such mystery
and will not tell us how or why or when.
It also doles out its magic moments to us mortals
lovingly, but sparingly.
Why?

You know what happened to Icarus.

Per Aspera Ad Astra

It was one of the Latin phrases
Mr. Lucas made us memorize,
right up there with the useful *morituri te salutamus*
and the ever-popular *poenas dare*.

Innocent marm that I was,
virtual virgin to life's bumps,
I viewed it as a clump of accusatives,
assonance, alliteration,
a lesson for the brain and not the heart.

To the stars through bolts and bars.

It was two summers later that
I suddenly saw the light,
as I locked adolescent horns with
David Benjamin in the finals at Powhatan.
Fist cramped to Kramer,
popping salt and feeling stars
much closer to me than victory ever seemed,
I could hear Lucas' raspy voice and see
his stern blue-grey eyes soldering the words
into our psyches.
And then, when the battle finally ended,
I realized his wisdom:
it was the struggle I cherished,
not just the triumph.

It should just be The Agony of Victory.
Period.
Since there is no real defeat, it being a great crucible,
nothing but a prelude to future victories.
And victory itself must be gained, struggled toward, grittily,
teeth clenched, through asperity.

Shun Fujimoto knew it,
bones broken but not spirit.

So did Ashley Cooper in '58
and Kirk G. rounding second
and Chang (vs. Skoff) at The Miracle of Vienna
and Willis in the Seventh Game.
But so did Branca and Decker and Buckner and Jansen,
surely no less noble in their quests.

The paradox is there, in front of our noses:
if only we could learn
to savor our setbacks, our struggles, our strifes,
which twinkle and shine beneath their dull façades,
so many constellations.

Between the Lines

A fine line indeed between
Sports and Life.

First, the issue of self-containment.
Baseline, foul line,
service line, side line,
red line, blue line,
goal line, yard line,
start line, finish line,
back line, front line,
line of scrimmage:
beginnings and endings,
goals and limits,
freedom and discipline.

Further: the beauty of it all
doesn't reside in the concrete,
in the throwing or the hitting or the shooting
or the catching or the passing or the chipping
or the serving or the punching or the jumping.
Nor in the coveted triumphs to which these are the means.

No. It resides between the lines.

In the groping and the struggling and the questioning
and the learning and the growing and the understanding.

Heard melodies are sweet, but those unheard are sweeter.
Winning isn't everything, it's the only thing.

Keats and Lombardi couldn't both be right.
Sorry, Vince.

THE LITTLE GUY

It's not the size of the man that counts; it's his height.
—Heading of my college stationery

They laughed at Veeck and called him clown,
they thought it was a joke,
that it made The Game a circus,
the day Eddie Gaedel
walked on four pitches.

The real joke: it was *they* who were the midgets.

I think it was Wilt who said
no one roots for Goliath.
(Or his descendants: Willard, Mikan, Liston,
The Dipper himself.)

So this is dedicated to:
Schantzie and Albie and Stu-off-the-mound
and Tricky Dick and Muggsy and Tiny and Spud
and Slater and Whitey and Calvin and Cooz
and Woos
and Dibbsie and Solly and Eddie LeB
(little Eddie LeB)
and all the second basemen out there.

Short may you live.

The Two Impostors

If you can meet with triumph and disaster
And treat those two impostors just the same…
—Rudyard Kipling

A month short of his seventh birthday,
the kid is perched in front of the seven-inch Dumont,
heart pounding like a Zollner piston,
hands pressed together
like an angel's in some Gothic altarpiece,
but praying for a miracle of a different order.

Clint Hartung is at third base, Whitey Lockman's at second,
the Dodgers lead 4-2, and there's one man out for the Giants.

DNA and destiny have conspired to make him
a Giants fan in Brooklyn.
One of the Chosen,
Israelite wandering toward hardball Canaan,
he casts his look of faith at the black-and-white spectacle,
makes a silent covenant,
and peers in for The Sign.
(C'mon, Bobby, you can do it!)

We're gonna stay right with it,
and we'll see how big Ralph Branca will fare
against Bobby Thomson, and then Willie Mays to follow.

This poem is about hope.
Pope's eternal-springing hope,
only the all-American version.
(C'mon, Bobby, you can do it!)
Anything's possible
in this best of all possible worlds.
Hey! This is America,
home of the brave,
where dashing, daring heroes
appear in the nick of time,

make things right again,
then ride off into the sunset.
Home of Roy Rogers. Dick Tracy. Mighty Mouse.
(C'mon, Bobby, you can do it!)

Jim Hearn is warming up in the bullpen—he's not
appeared in relief this year. Clem Labine is throwing
in the Dodger bullpen along with Carl Erskine.
And Bobby Thomson is on the biggest spot
of his entire baseball career.

This poem is about despair.
Who you kidding, kid?
This ain't the movies.
There's a sucker born every minute.
Lasciate ogni speranza, voi ch'entrate, kid!
Give it up: it's oh-and-one,
and Ralph's just setting him up
for the curve low and away,
then the high, hard one.
Hey! Doncha hear the P.A. guy
announcing Series tickets at Ebbets?
Even Leo will tell you:
these nice guys'll finish second.

Bobby has never been involved in a pennant race as yet.
This is the biggest spot of his entire baseball history,
and he'll be up there swinging against big Ralph Branca.

This poem is about victory.
In thirty seconds,
at exactly 3:58 PM,
Bobby will circle the sacks like a seven-year-old,
then touch home,
and his life will change forever.
And so will yours, kid,
and you'll start believing that winning is the Grail
and justice will prevail
and It's a Wonderful Life...

A home run will win it for the Giants and win the championship. A single to the outfield'll more than likely tie up the ball game and keep the inning going. So Leo Durocher comes over to talk to Bobby...

This poem is about defeat.
In thirty seconds,
at exactly 3:58 PM,
Ralph will bow his head in shame,
trudge to the clubhouse,
strike the Œdipal pose of utter disconsolateness
that Barney Stein will immortalize,
and his life will change forever.
And so will the lives of lots of kids, kid,
who, tigers no more,
will lead their kitten existences,
wearing their scarlet *L*,
never daring to risk.

Branca throws... there's a long drive...
it's gonna be... I believe...

This poem is about striving.
Rudyard was right as rain:
winning and losing
are mere illusions
posing as self-worth and inadequacy.
The *Tao* teaches us that
failure is an opportunity.
The real hero of this saga is Ralph.
Like the august Giants,
he never gave up on himself
and embraced his opportunity.
Like Job,
he learned faith and humility
from Bobby speaking out of the whirlwind.
Like Sisyphus,
he understood in time
the meaning of his burden

and never lost his grip on the rock.
Like the Bard's metaphor,
he was the poor player who learned
that strutting takes up the other thirty minutes.
Or,
perhaps he *really* throws the curve after all
or Bobby swings a millisecond late
or Gil plays six inches further to his right for Mandrake
and the game is over by now
or the wind picks up and Pafko snares it
or Sukey sends in Erskine instead
or Rube shakes off the sign
or Newk stays in
or Dressen walks Bobby to get to the rook.
Or,
perhaps, like Zeno's feathered dart,
that final toss never reaches its destination
and what we recall is only the striving,
the noble striving of fellow men,
the teeth-gritting, never-say-never striving
toward excellence and unfettered potential,
with no heroes, no goats,
no fame, no shame,
no impostors.

The Giants win the pennant!
The Giants win the pennant!
The Giants win the pennant!
The Giants win the pennant!

Mirror, Mirror

—For My Father

Who has stood over a three-foot putt,
and shoved or stubbed or pushed or pulled,
and not learned Character?

Who has gone for the green,
through hubris and two huge spruces,
and not learned Sacrifice?

Who has been buried in the sand,
inside a fried egg, behind a pine cone,
and not learned Humility?

Who has played behind
Bermudaed men taking forever
and not learned Patience?

Who has transgressed a rule,
in the interest of self-interest,
and not learned Honesty?

Who has nudged a ball from behind a root
to improve a lie (thus, to tell one)
and not learned Integrity?

Who has knocked a three-wood into the woods
when a five-iron would've done just fine
and not learned Limits?

Who has feathered a sand wedge
over a trap to within inches
and not tasted Immortality?

Meden agan. Gnothi seauton.
Nothing in excess. Know thyself.

Such were the teachings of the Oracle.
Such are the teachings of golf,
this mirror of life.

NIEDERHOFFER

Onto the court he schlepped,
late,
strange-named, strangely shod
in black Chuck Taylors
and shiny red basketball trunks.

On the other side of the net I waited,
punctual,
clad in polite Fred Perry whites
and immaculate Jack Purcells.

After the warm-up, a cosmic quandary:
how could nimbleness, athleticism,
etiquette, propriety, and orthodoxy
lose to
gawkiness, mind games,
nose-thumbing, crassness, and ambidexterity?

I kept it close the first set,
but in the end,
I beat myself, obsessed with the mindless dilemma
of form vs. function.

Could he be right?
Just get the job done. Even if it's ugly.
(What good is being correct in the jungle?)

Years later, I read about him in *SI*,
him!—challenging the Khans,
unheard-of feat in squash circles.
Perhaps they were thinking too much, as did I,
about BEATING THE FUCKER
and not enough about playing the game.

Mozart of his time,
against the grain and the Rules,
was it mere coincidence that his Christian name was
Victor?

HORSE

Leftie lay-up.
Leftie lay-up.
Rightie hook (backboard).
Rightie hook (backboard).
Push from 15 (swish).
Push from 15 (swish).
Set from top of the key.
Set from top of the key.
Leftie scoop (run-up from key, 360 twirl, swish).
H-O-R-S.
Underhand foul.
Underhand foul.
Driving reverse spin lay-up.
Driving reverse spin lay-up.
Pop from 20.
Pop from 20.
Fake short jumper, change in mid-air to baby hook (backboard).
Fake short jumper, change in mid-air to baby hook (backboard).
Over-the-head from 3 (no looking, overspin, swish).
Over-the-head from 3 (no looking, overspin, swish).
Half-court heave (no looking, no run-up, feet on the ground, swish).

I learned humility trying to keep up with Bobby Liss.

DEWEY DEFEATS TRUMAN

Branca K's Bobby, Bums Cop Pennant.
Hogan Humbles Fleck At Open.
Liston Pummels Cocky Clay In Lewiston.
Kentucky Five Too Mature For Miners In Final.
Riggs No Match For Court.
Joe, Jets Silenced By Super Colts.
Upstart Mets Swept By Birds.
Favored Russians Embarrass U.S. Pucksters At Placid.
Cal Almost Surprises Elway, Cardinal As Time Runs Out.

Hey, You Never Know.

BIGGER FISHES

L'amour-propre est le plus grand de tous les flatteurs.
—La Rochefoucauld

I'm not sure where the expression "hot shit" originated,
but that was me.

Dragging the albatross
of my high school scoring records around my neck,
I sauntered down the hill into the Purple Valley,
peacock in shorts,
to my first Eph frosh soccer practice.

Approaching the practice field,
I projected my goals-per-game stat
and envisioned my winning goal
against the Lord Jeffs in the season finale:
an overtime, over-the-head, tumbling, desperation bicycle,
a beaut that barely eluded the startled goalkeep,
ensuring my enshrinement in the
Ultimate-Freshman-World-Universe-Solar System-
Milky Way-Little Three Hall of Fame.

Until
I met the other guys who would make the starting eleven,
the Budges and Chips and Skips and Sandys and Randys
of the world,
all scoring-record holders and captains and superstars
at our nation's finest:
The Hun, The Gunnery, Andover, Exeter, Choate.
Hertzes, all, to my Avis,
and hotter shits.

The rest was history (theirs, not mine).
Yet I took away something
I still carry:
there may be bigger fishes out there,
but none who try harder to swim upstream.

RUMINATIONS

Homo Ludens

All work and no play makes Jack a dull boy.
—James Howell

Somewhere
between sex and thirst
is man's age-old urge
to play with a ball.

It must have started way back before the Greeks,
perhaps with Australopithecus,
who, after a long day
of trying to stay alive
and struggling with flint to start the barbecue,
invited a friend to come over to his cave and play.

Maybe they kicked a rodent's skull
back and forth across the front lawn.
Or, to relax and maintain their sanity
(in those carnivore-eat-carnivore days),
they might have tried hitting
woolly mammoth testicles with their clubs,
a kind of Cenozoic fungo.

And maybe a third wanted to join in,
uninvited,
and *saloogi* was born!
And then a fourth: running bases!
And then the whole cave complex,
as things got out of hand:
Pleistocene rugby!!!

And who knows?
Maybe back then,
way before Abner,
they discovered this neat game

(nine on a side),
kept stats,
gave out MVP's,
divided the caves into Eastern and Western divisions,
and formed a primitive version
of a players' union.

Biology Lesson

The human brain is comprised of
ten basic structures,
each with unique responsibilities:
medulla (breathing, heartbeat, waking, sleeping),
pons (dreaming),
reticular formation (brain's sentinel),
thalamus (relay station for sensory information),
cerebellum (bodily movements, posture, equilibrium),
hippocampus (long-term storage of information),
amygdala (aggression, feeding, drinking, sexual behavior),
hypothalamus (internal equilibrium),
cerebral cortex (higher cognitive and emotional functions).

And, present only in the confirmed sports nut,
the little-known *triviata minor*,
a tiny compartment that stores
information of no earthly value, like
Ted Lepcio's lifetime slugging percentage,
the NBA center born in Hilo, Hawaii,
and the name of the guy who tripped Dickie Moegle.

PALINDROMES

Pep.
Otto.
Seles.

All champions,
perhaps because when they
looked into the mirror, they saw
themselves.

MIDTERM

1. Why is the sky blue?
2. Which came first, the chicken or the egg?
3. Who was better?

(Was it Cobb or Willie?
Ruth or Aaron?
Hornsby or Rose?
Young or Koufax?

Oscar or Larry?
Cooz or Magic?
Elgin or Michael?
Wilt or Kareem?

Sayers or OJ?
Huff or LT?
Bronco or Butkus?
Baugh or Montana?

Howe or Gretzky?
Louis or Ali?
Hogan or Nicklaus?
Budge or Laver?

Apples and oranges?
Maybe.

But let's take away all the fancy equipment.
Equalize the training methods, the coaching, the apparel,
the money, the opponents,
leaving just the playing fields, plus
the intelligence, the mental toughness, the strategy,
the endurance, the grace under pressure,
the love of competition,
the will to win.)

OK, pencils down. Now for the answers:

1. The polarization of light, arising from the electromagnetic nature of light waves.
2. The chicken.
3. I dunno.

ON OPPONENTS

He brings out the best in me.
I respect him for the same goals I aim for,
the same qualities I honor,
the same standards I try to maintain.
Through hard work, courtesy, and the spirit of competition,
he is my brother, my mirror image.
So that when we both strive to reach a higher level,
in unison,
there is no loser.

Or,

that son-of-a-bitch
across the net
or on the other side of scrimmage
or guarding me
or staring at me from the mound
or lining up his putt
or moving his Queen's-side bishop
is threatening my security,
my sense of self,
my ability to succeed,
my integrity,
my pride.

God bless America.

UNIVERSAL LANGUAGE

A solitary shepherd is tending his flock on a Mongolian hillside.
A young woman goes to market in Tasmania.
A 90-year-old couple is making love in an Alaskan igloo.
A sailor orders another San Miguel in a Tierra del Fuego bar.
A trucker pulls in for some Java just outside of El Paso.
A teenager is constructing a spitball in a Brooklyn classroom.
And they all speak the same lingo.

Strike three! Safe! Home run! Yer out!
Good! Foul! Three! Yesssssss!
Touchdown! Complete! Tripping! Interception!
Corner kick! Penalty shot! Free kick! Goooooooooooal!
Ace! Match point! Fault! Let cord!
Fore! TKO! Wins by a nose! World record! Perfect 10!
Quadruple salchow!
He scoooooooooooooooooooooooooooooooooooooores!

Chess Quandary

The battle rages on: is chess a sport?

Consider this: sport at its finest requires
fitness and conditioning,
mental agility,
strategic intelligence,
an unswerving ability to focus,
and a willingness to struggle nobly,
under the greatest of pressures
and despite physical and mental fatigue,
against an able and highly competitive opponent.
To say nothing of superb hand-eye coordination.

Hmmmmmm...

Argument Against the Existence of a Supreme Being

Someone once figured out that in a title fight,
the journeyman heavyweight,
James "Buster" Douglas,
earned nearly twice as much *per second*
as the immortal Lou Gehrig did
during his most productive *year* in pinstripes.

Perhaps Nietzsche was right after all.

Memories

Spaldeen

Strutting out of Linick's Toys
with my brand new Spaldeen,
I imagine how grownups feel
prancing out of the showroom
with their brand new Caddy.

Pink and firm and fresh,
it expires that pristine odor of powder,
fosters feelings of well-being and desire.

I run home breathlessly, slaloming between
the DeSotos, Hudsons, and Packards
that clog Thirteenth Avenue
this April dusk, 1954.

Times were simpler then.
Before rock 'n' roll. Between wars.
Ike, Uncle Miltie, Spaldeens.

The ritual is always the same.
I am poised opposite
the brick wall in my driveway,
caught up in a world closed to other humans.
Oblivious to all: the occasional *Chassid*
peering in curiously on his way to *shul*,
the fruitman hawking his bananas,
stoopball games down the block.

My tools are ready too:
PM1, well-oiled pal I use for
liners, popups, grounders, and flies;
floppy first-sacker's mitt
that looks like Ollie,
but whose webbing catches everything,
Black Widow's abode that snares its victims
in a way Hodges and Power can only dream of;
Spaldeen.

I always have home-field advantage:
the Visitors never have a chance.
For I know the field far too well,
every nook of brick and cement,
every crack, every imperfection.
I am 4'8" and nine years old:
I know my limitations.
But somehow, against all odds, there is
no physical feat, no leap (of foot or faith),
no amazing play I can't make.

Now I'm ready. I put my Ernie Harwell voice on.

Now batting for the Phillies, number one,
Richie Ashburn.

(Boos.)

Antonelli, the cute lefty, winds up. He kicks.
He delivers.
Ashburn smashes a screamer in the hole...

My Spaldeen hits the wall, obediently,
precisely two inches from the ground,
then skitters to my left.
Impossible chance. Way too far to reach
before it passes me for a bingle.

But no!

Here comes Al Dark from out of nowhere,
backhands it,
pivots,
and pegs it across his body!
But the throw's in the dirt!

Switching mitts Houdini-like,
I peg Pinkie against the wall.
It ricochets crazily from a crack I know by heart,

lands inches in front of Ollie,
who calmly gobbles up the short-hop.

But Lockman makes an incredible scoop,
nipping Ashburn by a stride!

(The crowd goes wild.)

The innings proceed, play
following incredible play.
Mueller and Irvin and Mays leap to snare
towering flies by Ennis and Torgy;
Dark and Williams erase the occasional runner
with terpsichorean DP's;
Westrum and Thompson pounce on bunts.

The Giants lead, 1-0, on Willie's solo smash.
It is the top of the ninth.
I am a pool of sweat and must now transform myself
into Wilhelm while Hodges does
a Chesterfield commercial.

Now Russ is finished, Hoyt is warm,
and I am ready to close up the patient.
I fondle my Spaldeen,
position my two knuckles on top,
in the shape of a viper's fangs.

The rest of the story is not important.
I don't recall how it ends; it may
not have ended yet.
Perhaps my mother calls me in for dinner.
Or the green Chrysler pulls up:
Game Postponed Due To Parking.

But I prefer to remember the story
as I end it here,
my hand clutching my pink Spaldeen,
my heart as joyous as it has ever been.

Hangerball

Nature, shmature: it's *kids* who abhor a vacuum.

It was a sleepover at Jimmy Blumstein's.
The day had been competed away with endless games
that exhausted our ken:
one-on-one, horse, around the world,
stickball, stoopball, boxball, wallball,
sewer hockey, one-man punchball,
fungo.

But nighttime closed down
the outdoor ballparks
and brought with it parental requirements:
stay in your room, keep it down to a dull roar.

What to play *now*?
So, impelled by need,
we concocted Idiots' Delight.

HANGERBALL!

The Tools: wire hanger bent into a circle,
then wedged between door and transom;
old pair of Wigwam socks (white),
folded into a ball.

The Rules: no dribbling (!), but
you could fake-dribble.
Walking and double-dribbles allowed. No fouls.

The Fools: one lunatic wildly toting
a sock-ball in mid-air toward a floating hanger,
silently, earnestly.
The other, bumping, shoving, shadowing,
all over him like a rash.

It was all in the fakes, you see.
Left, right, then free for a scoop Guy Rodgers layup.
Right, left, then room for a hook from
Houbregs or Johnston or Kerr.
Fake in, then back up for a Gola push.
Until, after 4 hours, exhausted, in a heap,
we call it quits at 662-662.

Sometimes now,
when the world is too much with me,
I close my eyes
and imagine the two little maniacs,
passionate, focused, resourceful, creative,
their joyous universe defined
by that single instant of sock and hanger.

Paradise Incinerated

You did WHAT?

—Me (circa 1957, just after my mother
informed me that she had disposed of
my entire baseball card collection)

Midas? Croesus? Scrooge McDuck? I laugh at their riches,
pittances to my worth, had The Deed not been done.
An honest-to-God mistake, she claims.
Like a surgeon saying "oops!" claim I.

So, instead of living out my natural days
on my private, languid Mediterranean isle,
sucking on grape leaves and reading Proust,
I content myself with singing of lost treasure.

O Sibby and Alpha and Early and Ned!
With what passion I unwrapped you at the luncheonette!
And how, with deep breaths, I filled my face
with the gum powder that was covering yours!

O Sal and Erv and Ebba and Earl!
With what devotion and monk-like care
did I glue you with LePage's into the Log Book
with that black-and-white speckled cover!

O Coot and Cot and Gino and Sid
and Spec and Ruben and Elroy and Ike!
How painstakingly were you all arranged,
by team, position, average, ERA!

O Suitcase and Minnie and Wally and Turk
and Camillo and Ferris and Bobo and Gus!
With what fervor and focus did I flip you
(heads or tails, you landed obediently)!

O Dusty and Shotgun and Peanuts and Granny
and Vinegar and Birdie and Robin and Dee!
O Allie O Pumpsie O Virgil O Saul
O Carlos O Satchel O Reno O Clint!

Lost forever, but never in my mind and heart,
O how you haunt my dreams with your silly grins,
your studied poses, frozen rectangularly...
O Mother, how could you?

BEHIND THE BLACK CHEVY

Most of the details are long since faded;
there are no *madeleines* to recuperate them.

But sometimes, when I close my eyes,
I can see the scene on East Seventeenth.

Two-hand touch,
no blocking at the line,
no rushing until *five hippopotamus*,
touchdowns are the sewers,
out-of-bounds are curbs (not parked cars),
game ends when dinner is served.

Lunatic kids competing their asses off,
deadly serious yet with the
ferocious joy of youth
and the pre-adult, unadulterated
sense of commitment.

Hank, you go out five steps
and I'll hit you at the trellis.
Richie, buttonhook short down the middle.
Billy, fake short, then go deep,
and I'll hit you at the sewer.

But now Hindsight wags its finger at me,
pointing out my cruelty.
I spot our team's Fifth Man, with a clarity
conspicuously missing from the rest of the image.
(We needed a fifth to even out the sides.
He couldn't run, catch, or pass
but possessed the unassailable asset of availability.)

At every huddle, his instructions were identical:
go behind the black Chevy,
and I'll hit you if you're open.

Of course, he was always open
but never once touched the ball.

The reverie ends with him,
trotting back to the huddle, silent,
his sad dog-eyes begging for inclusion.

What is he today?
A neurosurgeon or novelist?
A homocidal maniac whose scars of youth never healed?
Or perhaps he's still standing, alone,
behind the black Chevy,
waiting for a pass to come his way.

Emerson Transistor

When they first came out,
the mid-fifties I think,
my folks got me one.

Black, Emerson in gold
beneath lint-catching plastic slits.

So cool to turn the tiny wheel a speck
and get Murray the K or Cousin Brucie.
Or to pop it in a pocket or a bag
and tote it wherever.

But best of all, there was the deception:
the perverse, methodical, premeditated plan
to defy my curfew.

(Was it Fate that weeks before,
I had discovered the joys of *Crime and Punishment*?)

Ten o'clock: lights out.
Maybe, but here comes trusty ol' Emmo,
quickly, furtively deposited under the pillow.

Volume up, so I can hear through the foam.
Not too much—could get caught.
I am living, on the edge, the life of some escapee
straight out of Stalag 17.
There: just right.

O, the sweet, sneaky, solitary sessions of sin
stolen between Ipana and slumber!
Ear pressed hard against pillow,
feigning innocence,
I am lullabied by the mellifluent tones
of the great Marty's Glickmanese:

Now it's Braun passing to Dick McGuire,
now back to Carl at the top of the key for a two-hand pop:
Gooooood! Like Nedick's!

Yes!

Now it's Dolph Schayes getting a pass from Seymour,
he slices to his right, he drives past Gallatin,
he lays it up, it's good and he's fouled!

Shit!

A few years later, it had survived,
battered and taped and crumbling,
but no less my accomplice in deceit.

Now it was Les Keiter
with his phoney, endearing re-enactments:
the *tock*! of bat against ball well after the fact,
the canned crowd roar,
the ticker-tape fueling my waning
but still fervid passion for the now-departed Jints.

How long ago, and how primitive!
Yet, in our world of remote control and replay,
how nice it is, now and again,
to hearken back wistfully
to the days of my little black Emerson,
the days of true adventure and derring-do.

PM1

I think it was April of '51
that the pleading finally paid off:
as forsythia and baseball
begin to sprout,
I drag Dad off to Davega's
for my very first glove.

From the row of Rawlingses,
the one on the extreme right
beckons like a Siren.
Succumbing, I pluck it from the company
of its nearly identical octuplets
and plunk down all my worldly savings.
It was twenty bucks
(you could get a Caddy then for four thousand)
and worth all 2000 pennies.

Like a new father
clinging to his precious arrival,
I cradle mine all the way home.
Exuding that intoxicating smell of cowhide,
it is healthy (thank God!):
all four fingers intact and perfectly formed,
umbilical knot (an outie) at the base of its thumb.

Then, the baptism.
First, anointing it in its ritual bath,
I perform The Soaking In Neat-Foot's Oil.
Next, The Diapering In Swaddling Twine,
as I wrap it tight,
hardball tucked snugly into nascent pocket.

With paternal pride,
I watch as it grows.
As it swallows up, with decreasing effort,
hardballs, softballs, tennis balls, Spaldeens.

As it perfects the arts
of shagging and snagging
and snatching and spearing
and scooping and smothering.
As it darkens and softens
and accrues character through rites of passage:
Marks By Spikes, Soaking By Rain, Bites By Dog.
Until, through it all, it transforms itself at last
from glove to Mitt.

Decades whizz by.
And there I am,
spending endless hours playing catch in the driveway,
first with Noah, then Jennifer, then Sarah
(the true products of my loins).
Fully grown,
I am filled this time with the authentic joy
of a real-life father
sharing past and present.

The joy is total, ineffable.
Except that I am using
some five-fingered Behemoth,
a ready-made,
pre-oiled,
pre-molded,
grip-tight,
power-snap,
snap-action-pocket thing
with no soul,
made in a hi-tech, cookie-cutter
factory in the Philippines,
a Ramon Martinez model.

Who is Ramon Martinez?

When Caucasians Ruled the Hardwood

They had names like George and Red and Vince
and Harry and Neil and Adolph.
And they played a game from another planet,
piper cubs to our Concordes.

It was before jumping was invented:
ten wan men standing still,
waiting for something to happen.

Like chessmen they moved, but no black pieces.
Pawns proceeding cautiously,
one square at a time.

Were they in college today,
perhaps they'd continue on to law school
or become accountants.
But then, they ruled the hardwood.

It was a gentler game then, domestic even.
When grown men had soft touches,
threw kisses,
pushed and set,
weaved and scooped and hooked.

Now, one explodes, crashes, penetrates, violates,
slams, jams, goes back door.
Then, the only underhanded act
was a charity toss.

A black-and-white snapshot I kept from those years
sums it up best:
as the acromegalic center strains upward for a lay-in,
the three defenders, babyfaced, startled, aghast,
but proud rulers of the hardwood,
stand there stiff, as if nailed to the floor,
spectating.

6/28/54

Thirty-nine years have passed,
and all I can remember is this:

Day game.
Jints vs. Bosox.
Annual exhibition.
Jints win (I think).
Westrum wins catchers' throwing contest
(into cannon behind second).
Willie and The Splinter have homer-hitting contest.
Willie wins (I think).
Paul Giel starts vs. Leo Kiely.
Both bonus babies, like Joey Amalfitano, who was there too.

My very first ballgame,
and you'd think I could come up with
more details, more names, more memories.

But to this day,
the only other things I have kept are
a foul ball my Dad caught off the bat of Davey Williams.
And a lifelong passion.

The Bunt (A Fairy Tale)

Once upon a time,
a very long time ago
(are you listening, my children?),
before the days of
seven-figure salaries and whining,
when men were boys
and loved the game
and were loyal to their teams,
there lived a wondrous craft they called
The Bunt.

And everyone throughout the land learned to do it,
so uplifting and majestic was its execution.
Even pitchers.

And they practiced this beauteous craft,
over and over and over,
until it became an art:
hands apart,
dominant one at the label,
thumb up,
pull bat back like you're catching ball.
Plop. Spin. Dead as a doornail.

The Bunt had nobility,
allowing for transcendence
and the suppression of the Self.
Descendants of Abraham
were these bunters all,
coming to learn the meaning
of the word *sacrifice*.

The Bunt had power,
the only purely peremptory play,
allowing the fielder no choice
but to throw to first.

The Bunt had magic, my children,
able—presto!—to turn
singles into automatic doubles
and harmless walks into rallies.

But then one day,
one terrible day,
along came big bucks and free agency and strikes
and Sloth and Envy and the DH Rule.
And in time,
like The Unicorn and The Egg Cream,
The Bunt vanished from the face of the earth.

The End.

First Kramer

Since then, I have owned others,
plus 55 or 60 Maxpli Forts,
a couple of Kneissel Aeros,
and 6 Yamaha Secret EX's.

But you never forget your first Kramer.

It was a Wilson Jack Kramer Autograph.
With Jack's autograph in script,
written right there on the neck,
above blue and red letters on white shaft
(*way* before the king's crown appeared).
Ligneous weapon from the noblest of trees,
when graphite was what they put in pencils.

They say the racquet doesn't matter:
Beppe Merlo proved it by crushing everyone in sight
with his dinky, red-handled, no-name job
strung at 22 pounds.
But in the days when balls were white,
there were racquets. And there were Kramers.

I wielded mine proudly till the day it died,
when,
battle scars racking its sallow body,
nascent warp twisting its noble face,
its upper torso badly beveled from digs and scoops,
its decals—shadows of their former selves—now reading
"J ck r mer,"
its worn grip sporting only desultory perforations,
the cotton "W" on its butt frayed to shreds,
I finally laid it to rest one sultry afternoon,
8/15/59.

Requiescas in pace, ol' Jake.

Ode To My Left Saphenous

—For Michael Feld

The first thing I recall after the operation
wasn't that I was almost a goner.
Nor the pain that racked my body,
then and just before,
nor the knowledge that a fifth of my heart was gone.

Instead, I was struck by
the 24-inch stapled snake
that meandered its way from left groin to left ankle,
Nile of my limb.

What had they done to it?
Would it ever be the same?

I thought back to all it had done,
pal-o'-mine.
Running (with its right companion)
bigger and stronger opponents around
on the other side of the net.
Pushing off for layups and buttonhooks.
Anchoring for forehands, penalty shots,
swings at the plate.

I remember how I listened,
in awe and in hope,
as the surgeon explained how they had
cut the vein into four pieces for the bypass.
How the pieces then had to learn to be arteries.
And how capillaries would
begin the miracle of compensation.

The scar has faded now,
but not the memory of that first day after,
when I lay, close to tears, staring at
The Little Leg That Could.

Portraits

SAY HEY

There have been only two geniuses in the world.
Willie Mays and Willie Shakespeare.
—Tallulah Bankhead

Those of little faith, those even who worshiped Baal
could not have invested
as much devotion in their idol
as I did in mine.

Willie!

As you awaited the train
in Birmingham (or was it Mobile?),
garbed in jacket, buttoned tieless shirt, silly brimmed hat,
a rookie's fear in your eyes,
could you have known that
you would soon wield the power
that all icons wield?

As you sat peeing in your pants
in the on-deck circle,
just before the man from Glasgow
swatted the immortal Shot,
could you have dreamed that
you would cause
a white Jewish professor-to-be
to slide into the pillow on his bedroom floor,
again and again and once again,
his right thigh throbbing with strawberries,
until he got the cap to fall off just right?

As you muffed Waitkus' fly
in your first game
and went oh-for-twelve to boot,
could you have supposed that,
kiteless Franklin reborn,
you'd discover electricity all over again?

Who cares about aging Willie the Met?
Or that guy who had to sell cars on TV?

Me, I care about
Willie of the Lost Cap,
Willie—back to us—plucking Wertz's blast into his basket
like a tuft of cotton,
Willie with his rump and hips and right thumb
itching to explode in the box,
Willie and his high voice
and twinkling eyes
and boyish glee.

Maybe Tallulah *was* right:
before or since,
no mortals could make a play
like those two Willies.

Wilt In Hershey

Stonefaced and stymied,
the writer sits at his desk,
left hand stroking his beard,
right hand tapping his Mongol Number 2
on the empty pad.

Nothing.

For weeks he has been trying
to father a screenplay,
something about sports,
something gripping,
a huckleberry ripple folks could escape to
in the midst of their vanilla.

And then,
without warning,
the light flashes on
in the thought balloon,
bringing with it The Ultimate Plot,
not in dribs or even drabs,
but full-blown,
like Athena out of Zeus's forehead.

Aha! Eureka! Yesssssss!
It will be a fairy tale,
he bubbles.
Something no one would ever believe,
light years beyond *Damn Yankees*
or *Field of Dreams*.
Something funky, fanciful, and fun.

Let's see.
The setting won't be a city,
but someplace Willy Wonkesque,
where they make chocolate bars and joy...
Hershey!

Next, I'll have one team score, uh, 147 points,
with *three* guys scoring over 30 apiece...
and LOSE!

OK, this is good, real good!
And the other team,
they got this giant guy who goes *bonkers*,
and he scores 70,
no 90,
no, wait...a HUNDRED points!
Yeah, that's the ticket!
This is great,
this is incredible,
I'll be rich and famous!

Where was I?
Oh yeah...and this giant guy
not only scores 100 points,
but y'see, in real life,
he can't hit the side of a barn
at the foul line,
like he's *awful*,
around 50% or somethin',
but in *this* game,
he's got like this magic touch,
he can't fucking miss,
and he ends up goin' 15 for 20,
no, 25 for 30,
no wait: TWENTY-EIGHT FOR THIRTY-TWO!!!

Naaaaaaaaaah...

CHANGING OF THE GUARD

It was a Nietzsche special, the '74 Open finals:
out of the ashes of one life was born
the beginnings of another.

The noblest of ancients on his pyre:
Muscles,
all etiquette and backhand,
who spoiled Lew's Slam in '56
and then, a fortnight of years later,
emerged from the greatest field ever,
Energizer Bunny with perfect hair.

The new guard itching to ascend:
Jimbo,
all power and vinegar,
rambunctious Bellevillain,
Pancho's Quixote on a quest
to slay Australian windmills.

Muscles wore green that day,
color of optimism and eternal growth;
Jimbo was in red,
color of fire and brimstone.

Everything pointed to Drama and Suspense:
old school vs. new,
finesse vs. power,
great champion vs. future one,
rightie vs. leftie,
conservative vs. radical,
Aussie vs. Yank,
two battlers
who never give up,
a sure-fire five-set, five-hour,
nail-biting, knee-knocking,
marathon fight-to-the-finish.

So, ladies and gentlemen,
sit back, fasten your seatbelts, hold on to your hats,
and get ready for one of the classic confrontations
in the entire annals of sporting competition!

The scores: 6-1, 6-0, 6-1.

The Man

Three things I feared most when I was a kid.
The dentist.
Brussels sprouts.
And seeing that red number 6 stride to the plate
against my beloved Giants.

Ray Jablonski and Frank Thomas used to kill us too,
but it was The Man,
all scrunched up in that crazy corkscrew stance,
who was the scariest.

Because The Man was gonna put a hurt on you.
If not now, next time up.
Double in the gap, usually.
And usually with plenty of men on.

Willie was more exciting,
Mickey had more power,
and Ted was a better hitter.
They were all men among men.
But none of them was The Man.

Stan was.

EVERYMAN

Was it the way you cocked your head after contact,
like a mother osprey, chicks at her breast,
reacting thoughtfully to the sound of danger?

Or the fact that you came from the working-class town
where they make Rolling Rock?

Or your knock-kneed putting stance,
awkward icon of struggle?

Or your swashbuckling gait,
loyal American going off to golfing war?

Or the heaving of caution to the wind,
the go-for-broke, can-do,
no namby-pamby, wishy-washy, should I-shouldn't-I
mindset?

What was it all those millions of people
in your loving Army saw in you?
(Jack was better, Gary was scrappier,
Lee was flashier, Tom was deadlier.)

Perhaps it was their own reflection.

Suspended

The traditional tale of Sir Isaac Newton
and the falling apple is of significance
for its stress upon the fact that
bodies tend to fall toward the earth.
They fall because they have weight,
and the cause of their weight is the
attraction that exists between the
matter of which they are formed
and the matter that comprises the earth.

Then along came Elgin Baylor.

THE BARBER

When all is said and done
and the books are balanced
and the record set straight,
they'll credit Niagara with two great products:
her majestic Falls
and The Barber.

Mineo was the rebel
and Hepatica soothed tummies,
but *this* Sal's specialty
was the close shave.

One-o'clock shadow
toeing the rubber,
stubble with cap and spikes,
he earned his keep
not with the accustomed tools
of orthodoxy: youth, power, speed, strength.
No. His was the path of cunning and intimidation.
For he was The Barber.

No razors or Barbasol,
just cut those corners with the cowhide,
brush 'em back with the roundhouse curve
aimed for the earlobe
(not too short in the back, Sal).
Nibble, nibble, slice, slice,
OK, kid, you're done: *next*!

His black-and-white in the Times obit
flicked on the switch of my Time Machine:
there I was, in front of the old Dumont,
listening to Russ's play-by-play,
watching The Barber toil and scowl,
hunched over in white uniform with invisible blue collar,
snarling in for the sign.

Pistol's Haiku

Faded socks flopping,
whirling dervish of the court
draws from the hip: *swish*!

EMPERORS OF DAYLIGHT

Three ways to get past the defensive line.

Over.
The master: the *other* guy who wore 32
to hide the "S" underneath.
X-ray vision allowed him to see the smallest of openings.
Explosive bursts let him leap over tall noseguards.
It's a bird, it's a plane,
it's Juice.

Around.
The king wasn't The King,
but a wiry puma with Gale-force speed
(#40 in your programs)
who wiggled, squirted, and juked
like a globule of liquid mercury.
He couldn't kill you by bludgeoning or explosion
but preferred Death By Tantalizing.

Through.
Domain of the *original* 32,
best ever at plowing.
Mack Truck with neither driver nor brakes,
he was the only NFL player ever
whose formal name (Mr. Brown)
had a double meaning.

The best way to reach daylight?
Depends on how you like to travel.

Dream Match

Forget about King vs. Riggs.
What I'd pay good money to see
is a 3-out-of-5er,
on *equal* footing
(same age, same rules),
between the following.

A woman
with the grace of Suzanne, Maria, and Evonne;
the athleticism of Althea, Martina, and Steffi;
the dominance of Helen, Mo, and Margaret;
the fire of Billie Jean, Chrissie, and Monica.

And a man
by the name of
Rodney George Laver.

Fischer King

What are the odds?

A kid from Erasmus in Brooklyn,
pariah, rebel,
eschews the trodden path,
the American hardball dream
to push, dark and solitary figure,
little black and white pieces of wood.

Fighting against his devils
and decades of Soviet rule,
pipsqueak up against The Power That Be
(the one that pays its pawns royally),
he blasts through the dogma, the bias, the rigidity
with his own agenda
and a talent that leaves sparks on the board.

Man without a country,
he astounds the world by grabbing the Grail,
then, like any self-respecting comet,
vanishes in a puff of self-destruction.

Karl Spooner of the chessboard,
Bobby, we hardly knew ye.

THE GREATEST

Cocky kids full of themselves:
a dime a dozen.
But brazen promises
backed up by heroic deeds:
as rare as an Indian-head penny.

So: I raise my proverbial glass to
the trio in my Pantheon of Talent and Tongue.

To The Sultan,
whose apocryphal index finger
preceded the Swat that,
hospital bed or no hospital bed,
inspired a nation to believe.

To the man from Beaver Falls,
whose equally well-documented (this time videotaped)
index finger
became the symbol of *chutzpah*
and hope for the Davids among us.

And to Cassius Marcellus,
Emperor of Brash,
whose mouth, agape,
screamed "I tole ya so!" to the world
over Sonny's inert body.

Some may have been better
(Ty? Honus? Joe? Willie?
Sammy? Otto? Sonny? Joe?
Jack? Gene? Joe? Rocky?).

But none greater.

The Other Babe

Thorpe. Mathias. Conley. DeBusschere. Ainge.
Wilt. Rafer. Bo. Deion.
Jim Brown.
No one-trick ponies,
they all possessed the amazingly rare talent
to *excel and succeed* in more than one athletic endeavor.
Yep, each one was sure as heck
Mr. Versatility,
a red-blooded all-American boy,
a guy that sorta made ya proud ta be a guy,
a fella that could bear,
with distinction and pride,
the title: *jock*.

And none of whom
could polish the spikes of another jock from Port Arthur
by the name of Mildred Ella Didrikson.

Who:
set records in swimming, high jump, skiing,
horseback riding, rifle shooting;
struck out Ruth and Gehrig in an exhibition;
was an all-American basketball player;
was a world-class champion performer in four major sports;
won eight events and tied for a ninth (baseball throw,
javelin throw, 80-meter hurdles, broad jump, high jump)
in the women's national track and field championships;
won two Olympic gold medals (world, U.S. records);
was the first female full-time golf professional;
won seventeen straight golf titles;
won the U.S. National Open and the All-American Open
after cancer surgery.

Man, oh man.

Jackie Nimble

Like some crazed insect's Dance of Death,
his nimble extremities jitterbug
to the dizzying rhythm of a killer.

The ritual is always identical:
premeditated, predetermined, precise.
The moth across the fie!d first casts
a peripheral glance at the blue-and-white blur
that dances back and forth,
back and forth.
Miraculously, the glimpse alone is sufficient
to decrease the metabolic rate.
Back and forth, back and forth again go the legs,
far too fast for the human eye.
Now, just as the moth's wings flap
to the set position,
they experience paralysis.
Law of Cause and Effect:
the brain, recognizing the predator,
is sending synaptic messages of fear
to the brachial muscles.
Extraordinary to see the venom
take effect without the slightest contact
between hunter and hunted.
The venom proves fatal:
the moth is frozen and helpless.

And its captor is free to fly to second base,
pigeon-toed,
just as quick as you can say
Jack Robinson.

About the Author

Bob Mitchell was born in Brooklyn in 1944 and studied at Williams, Columbia, and Harvard, where he received a Ph.D. in French and Comparative Literature. After teaching in France for a year on a Fulbright and an eleven-year career as a French professor (during which he wrote four books on French poetry), he went into advertising in 1981. In 1994 Mitchell worked in Tel Aviv as a special consultant on commercial film writing and production. He still teaches, both at the School of Visual Arts in New York, and at various colleges and universities, where he gives lectures and seminars on the creative process.

Passionate about sports, both as spectator and participant, he has been to every U.S. Tennis Open (Nationals) since 1951; has been a fan of all sports, major and minor, since that same year; has taught tennis professionally and still tries to play as often as possible; and also enjoys golf, baseball, basketball, stickball, platform tennis, and rollerblading.